I Can Feel Better:
A Tapping Story

I Can Feel Better:

A Tapping Story

"I Am Healing" Series

© 2014 Christy L. Anana

All Rights Reserved.

No part of this publication may be reproduced, stored in a retrieval system, or transmitted, in any form or by any means, electronic, mechanical, photocopying, recording, or otherwise, without the written permission of the author.

First published by Dog Ear Publishing
4010 W. 86th Street, Ste H
Indianapolis, IN 46268
www.dogearpublishing.net

ISBN: 978-1-4575-3472-0

This book is printed on acid-free paper.

Printed in the United States of America

Introduction to Tapping

I empower you to read this story when you feel sad, angry, overwhelmed, scared, or lonely. Notice how your body feels after you read the book. Read it as many times as you need to. Then, let other people read this book. As you feel good, then we can help others feel good. We can spread this feeling good to all people — and do our part to heal the world.

How I'm Feeling

I feel bad like I could break into pieces.

If I could give a number between 0 and 10 of how bad I feel, it would be 11.

Karate Chop Point

Even though I feel really bad, I deeply and completely accept myself.

Karate Chop Point

Even though I feel like I want to break apart into pieces and then disappear, I accept and like myself.

Karate Chop Point

Even though I wish I didn't feel this way, I accept myself right now and love myself.

Top of Eyebrow

I feel so bad right now.

Side of Eye

It's hard to breathe.

Under Eye

I want to feel better.

Under Nose

I've been through tough times before.

Chin

I am starting

to feel better.

Collar Bone

I am a good person.

Under Arm

I can connect with feeling good anytime I need to.

Top of Head

It's going to get better.

I want to feel good.

I can help myself to feel good.

Take a Deep Breath

Rate How You Feel...

Go back to your scale of 0 to 10, how do I feel?

If I'm more than 1, I'll go back and read the book again.

You Are Amazing

I see you! Do you know what a special, amazing person you are? You made it through to feeling good again. You can do this as often as you need to. Even though you felt bad, you made it back to feeling good. You got to experience that feeling and then you got to feel better. You are great! Look at you!!

About the Author

I am a National Board Certified School Counselor with a Master's of Education. I have a passion for helping children reconnect to a still and calm place where they are able to make choices for their highest good. As a school counselor, I guide students to communicate and regulate their emotions so they can be good friends and good students. I have found that when calming activities are done before a lesson, the teaching results are far better. As a parent, my children ask for my calming stories before they head to bed. It is a way for them to quiet the noise of their day and enter into deep relaxation. Tapping or Emotional Freedom Technique (EFT) is an amazing tool to help every person feel better.

You can find out more about me on my blog: christylynnanana@blogspot.com

CPSIA information can be obtained at www.ICGtesting.com
Printed in the USA
BVIW12n2006150117
473525BV00003B/11